A HISTORY
OF MY TATTOO

Also by Jim Elledge:

Poetry

*A Letter to No One Who Is Named "The Past" and the Thoughts That
Interrupted the Writing of It*

The Chapters of Coming Forth by Day

Four Chapters of Coming Forth by Day

Into the Arms of the Universe

Earth as It Is

Various Envies

Nothing Nice

Anthologies

Masquerade: Queer Poetry in America to the End of World War II

*Gay, Lesbian, Bisexual, and Transgender Myths from the Acoma to the Zuñi:
An Anthology*

Real Things: An Anthology of Popular Culture in American Poetry
(with Susan Swartwout)

Sweet Nothings: An Anthology of Rock and Roll in American Poetry

Criticism

*Standing "Between the Dead and the Living": The Elegiac Technique
of Wilfred Owen's War Poems*

Frank O'Hara: To Be True to a City

Weldon Kees: A Critical Introduction

James Dickey: A Bibliography, 1947-1974

Miscellaneous

A Student's Guide to Getting Published (with Susan Swartwout)

The Little Magazine in Illinois: A Directory

A HISTORY
OF MY TATTOO

A POEM
BY JIM ELLEDGE

2006

Printed on acid-free paper

First American Edition, 2006

Cover painting copyright © 1948; Paul Cadmus, *Playground*, 1948 (Egg yolk tempera on masonite, 23 1/2 x 17 1/2 inches [sight], Georgia Museum of Art, University of Georgia; University Purchase, GMOA 70.2619)

ISBN 0-932616-80-1

A History of My Tattoo has been manufactured in the United States and published by Stonewall, a division of BrickHouse Books, 306 Suffolk Road, Baltimore, Maryland 21218

Acknowledgments

The author gratefully acknowledges the editors of the following journals in which some of the sections of this book initially appeared, some in slightly different versions:

Indiana Review for "The Book of Toos," "Chamber of Mirrors," "His Silhouette Lurks Like a Panther's Against Jungle Foliage," "A Letter to No One Who Is Named *The Past* and the Thoughts That Interrupted the Writing of It," "'La Mamma Morta,'" "My Booty and Me," "Sometimes Little Red Riding Hood, Other Times Little Boy Blue," and "A Thread Common as Breath" and *Big Muddy* for "*Horror autotoxicus.*"

Street Lamp Editions, directed by Ryan Klos, issued "A Letter to No One Who Is Named *The Past* and the Thoughts That Interrupted the Writing of It" as a limited-edition chapbook of 100 copies, the first 26 of which were lettered A-Z and signed by the poet.

Many thanks also go to Brian Teare whose support of this volume has bordered on the heroic.

For David

Contents

...surely joy will outdistance
the century's mass graves,
the earth's furious junkyards;
surely joy will outdistance us.
—Cyrus Cassells

A HISTORY
OF MY TATTOO

Book I:
Lament for the Alien

His troops come together, and raise up their way against me…. He hath put my brethren far from me, and mine acquaintance are verily estranged from me. My kinsfolk have failed, and my familiar friends have forgotten me. They that dwell in mine house, and my maids, count me for a stranger: I am an alien in their sight.

—Job 19:12-15

"La Mamma Morta"

13 September 1997

On this, the downward
        slope of the old millennium,

a Saturday, late morning,
        sun shines its 72° on The

20th Century, and the silver
        sky spreads breezes blue

above green lawns below
        like any child's version of

creation. Sure, clouds puff
        along west to east and trail

shadows across continents
        mimicking shapes no child

would think to draw, in
        hues no child colors. The

20th Century knows sun's
        no hub and its rays no

splay of spokes. Most children
        disagree and trace it so

rolling through heaven—
                    never a flat tire or speed-

trap ticket. The 20th Century
                    knows, vaguely, sky's

limited, thinning way
                    way up there, into nothing

until not one breath of it
                    floats beyond earth's pull,

but there, too, children
                    argue, believing their silly

eyes, and so they color
                    blank page after blank page

the blue of God's sight
                    and stretch the sky before

themselves forever. *Forever*:
                    that beautiful word whispered

back and forth between
                    horny teenagers fumbling

in the back seat of daddy's
                    slick Caddy, wrestling one

another into a paradise of
                    touch and sigh and touch

again, then guilt's acid-tingle.

Forever: that terrible word

which, to The 20th Century,

means one edge of the page

to the next, the top of each

page down until skies meet

manicured lawns still dawn-

damp. Beyond the side-

to-side edges, beyond the

top-to-bottom edges, The

20th Century would fall off

the world—arms flailing,

mouth full of screams and

prayers—into the grinding

jaws of the unknown. *Look!*

The 20th Century thinks.

Grass trimmings stick to

everyone's Sunday shoes

—shiny, black, not a scuff

mark anywhere—in X's

and Y's. Someone slams

a limo's door, then someone

else, and they trudge up
           the hill's slope. Maybe a late

morning tea. Maybe cellos
           mooing through the slight

breeze. Maybe Timpani-
           like dew drops sparkling

through moaning strings or
           heat rising off a teapot

fog-like. *Look!* The 20th
           Century thinks. It's not

a yard like anyone's she
           knows—no bird baths, no

lawn ornaments (gnomes,
           flamingoes, geese, squirrels,

mushrooms), no red mailbox
           flags standing in the sky's

blue breeze; just lime head-
           stones, row after row

jutting snaggle-toothed
           out of the grass, and here

and there bouquets, dozens
           of plastic daisies, that most

sun-like of flowers, fresh
    through eternity. On this

side of the old millennium,
    no matter how often

The 20th Century's deaf
    and inbred neighbor yanks

his lawnmower's starter
    rope, its engine won't catch. It

coughs, sputters, wracking
    such a quiet neighborhood.

Maybe it needs gas, oil, new
    plugs, clean filter. Maybe,

so weak now her neighbor
    can barely stand on his

own, he just needs a hand.
    In the time it takes to say

Ahhhh at the doc's, grass
    grows knee-high. Moments

later, it's waist-high. And so
    on. Too late for The 20th

Century's neighbor. By now,
    grass chokes the mower,

wrapping its blades
　　　　　　around its blades—and tugs

once, then once again, but
　　　　　　tighter. Then suddenly

The 20th Century's shiny
　　　　　　pumps—never a scuff—stop.

An usher's lined chairs
　　　　　　into two rows, five chairs

each: plenty of vacancies.
　　　　　　No child would think to

sketch the tarp, the slight
　　　　　　mound it covers, nor the diggers

as they slung dirt out
　　　　　　of the hole they dug, not even

the diggers just after—as
　　　　　　they stood and surveyed their

job then leaned against
　　　　　　the backhoe, dabbing sweat

off their brows with red
　　　　　　bandannas they slipped

from their coveralls' back
　　　　　　pockets. The 20th Century

reaches into her pocket-
                    book for a smoke, thinks

twice about it before offering
                    me one, then snaps it

closed. Children do think
                    to add the hole darkness

haunts, its dank scent night's
                    perfumed whirlwind.

How deep six feet of darkness
                    is, children think, Crayolas

stationed midway between
                    the paper and their eyes

like space craft orbiting
                    a world theirs and not. We'll

never know whether
                    their crayons are poised and

ready to add more color
                    or poised and about to fly

away in horror. That's
                    why on the downward slope

of the old millennium,
                    after we've tossed handfuls

of dirt into the hole (as if we
>could fill it with two fistfuls

of dust), after we leave
>and follow our shadows home,

The 20th Century
>and I trace new lines star to star,

sun to sun, at night,
>reconnect the sky's pointillism,

a new skyscape stretched
>skin-tight over our heads

umbrella-like against each
>blow heaven delivers without

warning or pity. On this
>side of the downward slope

of the tired old millennium,
>the night sky's a hole

light-years deep The 20th
>Century and I stare into, holding

one another's hand,
>holding what's left of our lives,

holdingholdingholding
>what's left of our breaths.

My Booty and Me

New Year's Eve, 1979

After they swabbed & probed, after they
spread & prodded,
each gray
wishes me
mind-to-mind their version
of a smiley-face day—enough for a week!

     —& send me, still decked out in the
       Yoda jammies I wore to bed
          last night,
          back down
      a shaft of blue light knifed
    through the night sky & roof into a riot

of bodies that crowd & *I believe in*
miracles. Where you from,
you sexy
thang? drip
sweat onto a dance floor.
Too cool to care, no one lets on I've

    touched down as music throbs ceiling to
      floor, wall to wall, body to body.
         Darkness buds
         then blooms
      whiffs of amyl nitrite. Wedged
    among pumped pecs & rungs of sweaty

abs—centerfold perfect & in 3-D—hurts:
a good hurt, the kind one
really good
kiss will
Ooooh, love to love ya,
baby kiss away. The beat syncs with

        the strobe-light pulse. The disco ball's
            light spokes stir the fog
                machine's clouds
                    into dust
                devils that dervish into
        whirlwinds, that slip & slide helter-

skelter across the dance floor & wrap
each man belt-high then
higher as
they crowd
skin tight, one to one, one
against the next. My breath catches in

        my throat at the press of damp Dago-Ts
            & Lacostes in every pastel
                imaginable. Walls
                    of mirrors
                clone this claque of muscle
        boys into oblivion, one into the next, into

Jungle boogie, jungle boogie. Shake it
around. Jungle boogie, jungle
boogie. Feel
the funk,

y'all the next, & into the one after
him: the Christopher St. or Castro original

blurring into infinity. Tonight's HUNK-
A-THON! NIGHT at Klub
Déjà Voo
Doo &
tonight's guest M.C.? The
20th Century—in turns her best butch &

bitchy self!—backed-up by the house's
trio of G-String GuyZ. So all
the prettiest,
buffest *Every*
man wants to be a macho,
macho man to have the kind of body

always in demand boys climb down off
the pedestals they've each
built from
the shards
of one another's hearts &
unpout their day-job selves for hump-

night *cause boogie nights are always*
the best in town stardom,
a full
15 minutes'
worth. They wrap their
mustachioed lips around whistles

(those in the know blow cops' nickel
plate; wanna-bes kiss plastic)

        & tweet-

         tweet to

    the beat. The joke's on *That's*

  the way uh-huh, uh-huh them—on us—

& it's as dirty as mass graves left open,

their darkness deeper than

a child's

version of

midnight: We've already taken

the bait, swallowed the worm that Mr.

       Death dangles, the barbed hook it

         camouflages, bait so tasty,

              so easy

           going down,

        we don't even know it's

      snagged our *Push push in the bush*

flesh until years & boyfriends later. By

then, it's already too late.

But here,

at Klub

Déjà Voo Doo *You'd better*

knock, knock, knock on wood, we

      gyrate, set free onto the world at last.

        A set of keys dangles off

            one or

           the other

       side of our web belts, jangles

      SOSs *Have a little fun. Make a little*

love. Get down tonight to strangers &
comrades alike, catches
the light
as each
man on the floor dances with
himself, with each of his selves sweating

> on the walls as back-pocket bandannas
> in every color created flash
> one or
> another desire
> to those in the know. It's at
> that moment, when I see the signaling

—all of it quicker than Morse code,
more subtle than a gesture
or word—
that I
finally *Ahhhh, freak out!*
Le Freak: So chic! decide. I'll dress 50s,

> all poodle-skirt & beehive, sing girl-
> group numbers from
> Annette to
> Lesley, Shangri
> -Las to Chiffons, about
> each captain of the team who slipped

away like sand between my perfectly
manicured nails, about
how unfair
parents can

be, especially when it
comes to dating, about worrying over

which outfit in my crowded closet to
wear—songs penned when
a girl's
best friend
would gladly brand her *Ahhhh,*
shakeshakeshake, shakeshakeshake,

shake your booty with a bad rep for
just one lousy hickey,
much less
for going
all the way. & so, to
rhyme with *lass*, or maybe *loss*—I can't

now for the life of me remember which—
I took a deep breath, the
deepest, most
important one
of my life &, looking at the
disco ball above me, christened myself Cass.

Horror autotoxicus

Today, drawn beyond the White House nestled
     between sky and lawn, where carpenters
     saw, hammer, then raise bleachers into
place along Pennsylvania Avenue for Clinton's
second swearing-in, drawn along tree-lined
     boulevards, then past the Washington
     Monument and Reflecting Pool to
the Vietnam Veterans Memorial, my silhouette

grazed names, ranks, birth and death dates etched
     in the shiny, black wall, Mr. Death's
     graffiti: Elledge Don Thomas Capt
AR 05 May 36 18 Aug 66 / Elledge Keith O'Neil PFC
MC 10 Nov 47 14 Dec 66 / Elledge Michael Stewart
     1 LT AR 24 Oct 46 24 Jul 68 / Elledge
     Wayne Clarence PFC AR 29 Dec 49
13 Oct 68. I copied the four end-stopped lines off

a tome bolted down against theft near the Wall,
     excerpts from the epic that defines
     one shard of my generation the way
a window frames one mountain of the range
beyond it. Mr. Death could have scribbled
     in felt pen: Older gent ISO young
     guys for good time Race & cock size
unimportant Must be willing to go all the way.

No one minded her aerobics drag—spandex
    top to bottom, head and wrist bands,
    Nikes—the sister of a boy not named,
ranked, or dated. "He got home OK, as whole
as anyone did from Nam," she told the old
    VFW volunteer who answers visitors'
    questions and helps tourists find dead
boys on the Wall. "But he…." She took a breath,

then on tiptoe, stretching her right arm, felt
    the precise bare facts above her
    head too high for her to read, each
fingertip caressing his name, rank, dates. "…he
was my brother's friend, my brother's best
    buddy. They went in together—
    in the buddy system. My brother's
never come here. He swears he never will."

·

Buddy system: At attention, shoulder to
    shoulder, drunk on the nearness
    of flesh to flesh, closer to one
another than brothers, more distant than
lovers, saluting in their crisp, clean uniforms,
    they combined. Each one blurred
    into the next until no one knew
where one man ended and the other began.

·

The old man nodded, eyes half-closed, as she
    rattled on, gossip not memorial.
    Her spandex reflected a smear of
afternoon sun back into the cyclops sky.
His crimson fez bobbed—a bottle cast by the sole
    survivor of a sunken ship and full
    of SOSs onto an ocean iced with
light. Not a word, not a single, common

thread of sunlight for Don, Keith, Michael, or
    Wayne, not today, not for decades.
    Their deaths angled into my life
as easily as a hypo between layers of flesh,
the way the Walls' two wings meld seamlessly
    —planned, built, anchored, flightless
    —each boy blurring one into the other
then into my silhouette without my consent.

•

Buddy system: Two lay close as breath, uniforms
    flung onto bushes—the arms of one
    shirt circled the waist of the other,
pants inside out, one pair inching into the other
    —combined: one into one, the second into
    the first. *Baby*, one said. From where
I stood, I couldn't tell which. Night
filled the sky full of no stars and no moon.

Because night lay vacant everywhere you
    looked in the jungle, they filled it
    to brimming over with one another.
One said, *Baby*. Then *baby* again. His voice
caught. *O* bubbled from the other's throat,
    then his breath rushed free: *Baby-*
    babybaby. Then: *Shhhh* from one
or the other, I couldn't tell which, final as death.

Metaphor, camouflage: boys' blood blossoms
    from wounds springing bud-like
    into flowers; boys machine-gun
other boys' bodies into a mime-troop dance;
mines tripped, boys' souls wing heavenward,
    mindless of Mr. Death, a civilian
    who cradles scraps of their bodies
in his icy hands, drooling over sweet flesh.

Buddy system: Metaphor, disguise: a way
    to say I love you; a way not to say
    I love you but to mean it all
the more or just the same or not at all;
just another way to help a guy out,
    a helping hand to get off, to get off
    and out of the goddamned jungle,
away from dodging bullets for a few minutes.

No metaphor resurrects the dead, no disguise
    consoles those who live beyond them,
    no camouflage hides the living
from themselves. Nothing for the buddy who
escaped the system, for the cousin who moves

them and himself together, combining
one into one until who's who blurs like
here and there in a fog in the night in the jungle.

•

What's left of them: a litany of letters, a sum
of numbers, no different than
for anyone else on this sweet
and dangerous planet. Good little soldier boys,
good little soldier boys, good little soldier boys
—all of us—now they're dead
and gone. Happy happy happy
nineteenth, Wayne. Or is it your forty-seventh?

Book II:
Private Skin

I am weary of my crying: my throat is dried.... They that hate me without a cause are more than the hairs on mine head: they that would destroy me, being mine enemies wrongfully, are mighty.... I am become a stranger unto my brethren, and am an alien unto my mother's children.

—Psalms 69:3-4, 8

A Thread Common as Breath

11 October 1996

"Careful, Cass. Don't drag your skirts,"
Mother Camp—La Crymosa
her Christian
name—joked
with me in a voice thin
as moonlight. All day, I'd wheeled

Mother Camp's chair up one boulevard,
down the next, forty-three
of sixty-
six acres
of The Quilt left to visit
after lunch, each panel six feet by three,

a burial plot's specs. Maybe clouds filled
that late, autumn morning
sky, maybe
sunshine. I
don't recall. I do recall
how The Quilt spread all the way down

the Mall, Washington Monument to
the Reflecting Pool in a riot
of color.
Its messages
at once private & public.
I recall how someone behind us

chanted, "A prey of divers colors, a prey
of divers colors of needle-
work, of
divers colors
on both sides, the needle-
work praying"—a cheerleader boosting

        team spirit, a stalker fueled with a lust
            for men in dresses, or a street-
                smart evangelist
                  pointing out
            shortcuts to Heaven. "Don't
        look back," Mother Camp warned me,

her voice comet-tail-thin. "You'll only
encourage him." His voice
tracked us
around one
block of panels, then others,
the same litany—"A prey of divers

        colors, a prey of divers colors of needle-
            work, of divers colors on
                both sides,
                the needlework
                praying…"—over & over
        until it thinned to a whisper & he

vanished. Seventeen years ago, the
New Year's Eve we met,
at Klub
Déjà Voo

Doo, I'd stumbled into
the upstairs bar, where Mother Camp

      held court, soused to the gills on the
           freedom of my first gay
               bar. Years
               earlier, Mother
          Camp stopped being Justin
   Marks, 1 LT, USMC, two tours in Nam

under her belt. (Only God & her doctor
knew what else hunkered
down there!)
Discharged, Justin
spent half a decade in
wholesale, a buyer for a sporting-goods

      chain, & cruising the Boys' Town of
          one city or the next. Then
               she birthed
               herself almost
          weekly into a series of selves,
   a child's string of cut-out paper dolls, &

a few months before meeting me, she'd
abandoned electrolysis, let
her beard
go, took
to donning habits, & gave
birth to her last self: Mother Camp, Diva

      of the Nunnery, Last of the Immaculate
          Miss Conceptions. To

grocery boys
or valets
who stared, she'd ask, *So
much more classy than muumuus,*

don't you agree? Not long after we met,
she sat me down & taught
me self-
portrait: daubs
of rouge, touches of powder,
smears of lipstick, swipes of mascara.

"More Than a Woman" boomed from
the bedroom stereo & filled
her third-
floor walk-
up, a tiny apartment. My old
face blurred into a new one. It rose

moon-like across the triptych mirror's
middle panel. Mother
Camp's rose
beside mine.
"Lovely," Justin Marks &
Mother Camp chimed in, a hint of

crow's-feet shadowing their smile, a
pesky fly nose-diving me.
But today,
the last
time they'll spread all the
The Quilt out, every panel's SOS sent

skyward, a week before she'll die, her
body a traitor to itself,
Mother Camp
whispers the
best of its one-liners to me
as I scribbled them down for her in a

      stenographer's tablet: "He was heavy
            into hard-core bonding,"
                    "Beam me
                    up, Scotty,"
            "Fuck art. Let's dance,"
      "Call collect," "When I go, I want the

Winter Garden. I see a few sensitive
speakers—& then Siegfried
and Roy…."
& that
night, bedded down in a cheap
motel, Mother Camp tucked into the

      twin beside me, I dreamed *A spool*
           of thread long as earth's
                  orbit. A
                  needle. A
          blinkless eye. Fingers all
      bone & so bloody. The panel: glitter &

lace. Satin. Silk. A trim of leather. Perfect
in its two dimensions, thus
life-like.
Bloody whorls

of fingerprints polka-dot
satin & silk. The needle jabs. One layer,

> *the next. Pierces one nerve, the next,*
> *the one after it. Each nerve*
> *squirms, coils*
> *of them*
> *alarmed under the skin*
> *crackle & hiss & spit. She sews wearing*

Mother Camp's gown, its slit up the
back: wings folded. "Even
blind dwarfs
could see
it's nothing like the Teddy
I ordered," Mother Camp cackles.

> *Dizziness. Vomit rises up her throat.*
> *Fingers raw bone & bloody.*
> *One vein*
> *ripped open.*
> *Spits blood skyward, at God's*
> *one good eye. That falls, splashing, into*

letters at the foot of the bed. She pieces
them across the panel, so
many simple
letters, that
become simple words,
simple as breath: SEMPER FE FI FO FUM.

> Awake, I only recalled citizens crowded
> outside a castle, held torches

aloft, waved
nooses against
a child's version of midnight,
& insisted that I hand over the monster.

A Letter to No One Who Is Named *The Past* and the Thoughts That Interrupted the Writing of It

21 June 1963

My Dearest T.P.—
    He was already naked, and I
    said yes, caught up in the whorls of
his fingertips. I said yes to him
clearing his throat. I never thought
    once, much less twice. My clothes
    vanished in the blink of an eye. I never
touched a stitch. I said yes, and yes,

•

I was almost thirteen. Buddy whispered,
    Shhhh. Don't tell
    anyone. OK?
as each star rearranged itself. *Shhhh*, I
replied, my finger flush against his lips.
    Then I removed it and licked salt
    from his upper lip, from his
chin, down his neck, across his

•

yes, again. He pulled me close as skin,
    as breath and pressed his onyx and gold
    signet ring against my skin, its Gothic
J embedded on my upper thigh, one
of my hips, close to a nipple. *Branded,*
    he'd say. The gold of the initial like
    moonlight against an onyx sky. His
eyes filled the room full of want. Yes,

•

I was almost thirteen. Buddy whispered,
    Shhhh. Don't tell
    anyone. OK?
as each star rearranged itself. *Shhhh,* I
replied, my finger flush against his lips.
    Then I removed it and licked salt
    from his upper lip, from his
chin, down his neck, across his

shoulders, the right one then
    the left, from the right to the left
    nipple, and more. He said—
or maybe it was I:
I never
    could tell, after the first time, where
    I began and he ended
—*Shhhh.*

•

yes, to the tip of his tongue that
    etched whole sentences of want near
    my left nipple, down and across my
neck, to my inner thighs, yes to his teeth
that nibbled my lips and ear lobes
    until they burned, the backs of my
    knees and insides of my elbows
until he raised goose bumps. I said, yes

•

I was almost thirteen. Buddy whispered,
    Shhhh. Don't tell
    anyone. OK?
as each star rearranged itself. *Shhhh*, I
replied, my finger flush against his lips.
    Then I removed it and licked salt
    from his upper lip, from his
chin, down his neck, across his

shoulders, the right one then
    the left, from the right to the left
    nipple, and more. He said—
or maybe it was I:
I never
    could tell, after the first time, where
    I began and he ended
—*Shhhh.*

He said, *Don't tell anyone. OK?*
    I echoed, *OK?* I ad-libbed, *Please?*
    He smiled big as a god in love
and slid his arm across my chest
to my waist and drew me
       closer, the scent of his flesh welled
       up flood-like and veiled the stars,
a wave sent from God to the very

•

Yes, mine, he said, lifting me up
       into the afternoon sunlight, twirling
       me, flinging my shadow all
over the room. I'd look into his
face turned up as he lowered me, my
       chest flush with his, our breaths
       combining, and him or me,
I never knew which, saying, *Yes*

•

I was almost thirteen. Buddy whispered,
    Shhhh. Don't tell
    anyone. OK?
as each star rearranged itself. *Shhhh,* I
replied, my finger flush against his lips.
    Then I removed it and licked salt

from his upper lip, from his
chin, down his neck, across his

shoulders, the right one then
    the left, from the right to the left
    nipple, and more. He said—
or maybe it was I:
I never
    could tell, after the first time, where
    I began and he ended
—*Shhhh.*

He said, *Don't tell anyone. OK?*
    I echoed, *OK?* I ad-libbed, *Please?*
    He smiled big as a god in love
and slid his arm across my chest
to my waist and drew me
    closer, the scent of his flesh welled
    up flood-like and veiled the stars,
a wave sent from God to the very

best sinners on earth. *Shhhh,* I
    said, but he kept groaning. *Shhhh,* I
    echoed, not meaning it. *Please?*
I said, then, *It's my turn,* meaning
that more than anything
    else I'd ever said, or would ever
    say in my life. *Shhhh,* he said. *It's
your turn now,* he added. *Please,*

•

yes again, as light from the afternoon
    sun spilled through the windows,
    curved over, haloing his head as he
reared back, his mouth wide open and
deep as a cave, as sunlight splayed
    cross his shoulders as they rose and
    settled, rose and settled, over and over
over me, as he said, *Yesss.*

•

I was almost thirteen. Buddy whispered,
    Shhhh. Don't tell
    anyone. OK?
as each star rearranged itself. *Shhhh,* I
replied, my finger flush against his lips.
    Then I removed it and licked salt
    from his upper lip, from his
chin, down his neck, across his

shoulders, the right one then
    the left, from the right to the left
    nipple, and more. He said—
or maybe it was I:
I never
    could tell, after the first time, where
    I began and he ended
—*Shhhh.*

He said, *Don't tell anyone. OK?*
    I echoed, *OK?* I ad-libbed, *Please?*
    He smiled big as a god in love
and slid his arm across my chest
to my waist and drew me
        closer, the scent of his flesh welled
        up flood-like and veiled the stars,
a wave sent from God to the very

best sinners on earth. *Shhhh,* I
        said, but he kept groaning. *Shhhh,* I
        echoed, not meaning it. *Please?*
I said, then, *It's my turn,* meaning
that more than anything
        else I'd ever said, or would ever
        say in my life. *Shhhh,* he said. *It's*
your turn now, he added. *Please,*

he begged as he climbed on,
        his body a sky hanging over me,
        his sweat glistening in moonlight,
a splay of stars, a galaxy so close
I could taste its light, bathe in its light.
    Be my buddy, he said. *Be*
    you? I asked him. *Shhhh,* he said,
and his skin stretched over me was heaven.

                   •

How could I know then what I know now:
    younger boys, prettier boys, more
    experienced boys lounge around
every corner like cocked pistols. How could I
know then, as his body beat against mine,
    a wing against the sky, what I
    know now: This is as close to love
as I'd ever get the rest of my goddamned life.

Sometimes
Little Red Riding Hood,
Other Times
Little Boy Blue

New Year's Day 1980

With a flourish of a ball-
            point pen, The 20th Century

signs her name, each
            letter aflow with curlicues,

in the autograph book
            a fan who waited backstage

for hours held out to her
            with a *Please?!?* Then flipping

to the next page, he signs
            again in concrete-block-like

letters, as if after tonight's
            show he's unsure where

she stands. Maybe leaning
            against a Mustang, flicking

his cigarette butt into the
            dark sky and shifting his

weight from his left to his
                    right hip, his best come-

hither stance, or stopping
                    beside that same Mustang

to hike her skirt over her
                    left thigh, snap her garter,

and tossing her hair, drop
                    the skirt back into place. He

straddles the fence between
                    a patch of grass over here,

another over there,
                    the differences between blurred

as if someone's caged The
                    20th Century in a chamber

built of mirrors: The 20th
                    Century ceiling to floor, wall

to wall, reproduced glass
                    after glass, pane after pane

to the millionth power: The
                    20th Century but someone

not The 20th Century. From
                    here, even I can't tell

who's who, one joined
                to the next paper-doll-like,

the space separating one 20th
                Century from the next:

the breadth of a breath plus
                the Milky Way's circumference.

The 20th Century's forgotten
                whole months of his

life. Nose bleeds began
                the morning of the Night

of Lamentations, as she
                calls it in her diary: hundreds

by now. A grin-shaped
                scar near his left nipple—

a mystery to her and her
                mamma. A nebula-like

blotch stains his right
                thigh. No rhyme or reason.

Whole weeks of The 20th
                Century's life have vanished

without a trace, up
                in smoke, down the tube, just

like that: snap, voilà.
                The 20th Century claims it's

boredom, swears it's
                amnesia, prays it's not alien

abduction. Even now,
                she burns the hall light all

night, afraid if she gets up,
                she'll run into her mamma's

ghost lurking in the dark,
                her mamma's dentures

chattering in her left hand,
                and her right index finger

curling back and forth:
                Come here. Come over here....

Still, he's the buffest, butchest
                boy at the Klub Déjà Voo

Doo, the champ at throwing
                her shadow cloak-like

over the dance floor. Quite
                the chevalier, The 20th Century

doffs his plumed cap, bows
                from the waist, and queen

after queen swoons, drools, lines
        up for a peck—*Who* could

resist?—and to cop a quick
        feel, a conga line of the choicest

and the oh-so-very not-so-choice
        butt-to-groin: a vine of Sodom.

Democratic to a fault,
        The 20th Century never had

a type. Q-and-A'ed, she
        might admit anyone, trade

to troll, would do. Some
        nights, The 20th Century

appears at last call, lisping
        a Transylvania accent so thick

no beef cake breathing
        on this planet could hammer

a wooden steak through
        it. Other nights, beating the DJ

to the joint, she's pure
        surfer dude, all *like* and *cool*.

Still day or night or in
        between, The 20th Century's

just as happy to don
                a jock strap and nipple stud

as a teddy and pearls—
                Frederick's of Hollywood á la

International Male—but only
                if it's he and she center stage.

Book III:
On the Shores of the River Chebar

I have been an alien in a strange land.

—Exodus 18:3

His Silhouette Lurks
Like a Panther's
Against Jungle Foliage

21 December 1967

Thomas Johns, called Buddy, my favorite
        cousin, four years older, bunked
        in my room off and on most
of his adolescence. I gave him the twin
and took the roll-away. Then hard-up for
        fun in our one-horse town,
        he signed up for Nam. Two years
later, he came home. Not a scratch. One of

the few lucky ones. "I ain't never going back,"
        he recited too loud at the party
        the night of the day of his honorable
discharge. "Puddles of piss and piles of shit's
all I left in that hell-hole." The men guffawed,
        the women twittered. Their joy rushed
        the house, looking for hostages.
Their Good-to-have-you-homes mingled

with Christmas carols off the Magnavox hi-fi
        as they left, staggering to their cars
        around the life-size Nativity scene
outside with piped-in *bahs* and *moos*. In our
room, Buddy cleaned up to celebrate
        with his buddy also fresh out

of the jungle. He took his time
toweling off after a shower, twice over each

arm, three times over the rest of his body until
    I couldn't stand it anymore and
    turned away. He slipped behind me,
his body heat rising off him, fog-like off a jungle
floor. "You're surrounded," he said, netting
    me with the towel, pulling me
    to him. "Drop your guns and
come out with your hands up," he whispered,

dropping the towel, his arms around me,
    then: "You got tall and lean while
    I was gone." Maybe Buddy said,
Kiss the skin off. Maybe I did. Maybe he said,
Fingers do long division in just the right places.
    Or maybe the moon eaves-lodged,
    or the ailanthus at attention along
the drive, or the breeze brushing the window

did. But *his* hands were expert at my buttons,
    my belt buckle, the elastic of my
    church whites. Still behind me, his
breath scurried over my neck and drew shivers
over my flesh. "You a welcome-home present
    or Christmas gift?" He lifted and lay me
    on his uniform stretched like a third
guy across the twin bed he left two years earlier.

•

Bud: a flower before it blossoms, what bursts
       forth into something beautiful
          —a scent, a color, a texture, a touch,
a taste, a sound—like the Ugly Duckling whose
life so depends on later. *Buddy*: a friend, he
       who doesn't bring even one flower
       but something better in secret night or
day, something close to love...all over the place.

•

I woke the next morning to a nose bleed, the first
       of hundreds more, smeared over my
       upper lip, dripping into my mouth,
warm as Buddy's breath across my face, warm as
his arms wing-like around me the night before.
       I woke to my parents at the kitchen
       table. They didn't mince a word.
During the night's fog, Buddy and his friend
drove up an exit ramp head-on into a semi.
       That night, each star fell one by
       one, one by one, one by one.
I hadn't seen them fall. I was asleep, my nose
bleeding across the pillow and sheet into my
       mouth. Buddy's breath Buddy's
       breath Buddy's breath. He
whispered, *Shhhh. Don't tell anyone. OK?*

•

My father telephoned his brother's near-deaf
    neighbor, the only one with a phone
    for miles around in the foothills
of that part of the Missouri Ozarks. The neighbor
agreed to relay a message: *Berdell called. Lynnore's*
    boy killed. Car accident. Funeral
    Thursday. The old man heard:
Lynnore called. Berdell's boy killed in a car

crash. Funeral Thursday. To Uncle Alton
    and Aunt Vonda, to their children,
    and their children, I'd already
been dead three days when, late because one
car in their caravan of four broke down, they
    drove to our house not the cemetery,
    pulled into the drive, and parked.
Uncle Alton got out first, walked to the door,

and saw me only as he reached for the knob.
    His face warped into a knot as he
    stumbled back down the stoop.
Horror replaced the grief on his face. "Buddy died,"
I said, "not me." Relief then grief. Some days
    even now, decades later, Uncle
    Alton gets fuzzy-headed, combines
his two nephews, Buddy and me, into one,

the distance between Buddy and me blurring
    like the breath we once passed
    him to me and back to him, like
there and here in a fog in a jungle. Some
days, some nights, decades after the fact, I'm

blinded by a semi's brights, I'm
slamming the brakes, leaving two
skid marks double-crossing the Ts of *eternity*.

Chamber of Mirrors

31 December 2000

The 20th Century wheezes
                    up each flight, stops one

moment at the next-
                    to-the-last landing, a riot of

shadows. She pats sweat
                    off her brow with her

mamma's lace hankie,
                    her only inheritance, careful

not to smudge her
                    makeup, and sighs once, twice,

then continues the climb. Her
                    pumps' footfalls echo

in the stairwell among
                    children's laughter and curses.

They swarm outside,
                    playing touch beside the life-

size Nativity scene
                    in the unseasonable warmth.

The 20th Century turns
> her head—so polite! what

one'd expect from someone
> her age and breeding—

and leaning her walking stick
> against the banister, she

coughs a shallow cough
> from her throat, not her

lungs, into her cupped
> hankie as she'd done earlier

this afternoon at the
> proctologist's. In his office, she

listened as *Seven lords a-leaping!*
> *Six maids a-milking!*

in voices male and female
> rose, rounded the corner,

drifted up the hall, slipped
> under the office door,

wafted across mildewed carpets,
> then under a second

door into the doctor's favorite
> exam room, the one with

a wooden table—no cushion,
           only tissue paper that rustled

when she got on, rustled
           as she coughed, and stuck

to her butt when she got
           off. The 20th Century reaches

her apartment landing,
           the building's last, its highest,

and in the dim light,
           forages in her beaded clutch

for the apartment key. She
           coughs again. Perhaps this

time blood's in the hankie,
           not phlegm. It's too dark

for me to see from here.
           The key's slipped between

a compact that leaks
           powder and a cigarette case

she bought in some
           antique shop, its monogram

a floral initial *J*—
           not her initial. Not even mine.

To this friend or that
        foe, she'll claim it belonged

to a former beaux
        —one Hans, one Hong, or one

Ramón. Her favorite
        fantasy: a houseboy—sometimes

Günter, other times
        Kim Lee or Eduardo, always trade

—senses she's home
        and swings the door wide open

for her with a bow and
        flourish, dropping a cape she'll

walk upon as if
        keeping her from muddying her

dainty pumps. Except
        for the cape, he's nude, his abs

a ladder she'll later climb
        up or down depending on her

mood—or his whim. But now,
        no dream lover: no cowboy,

no cop, no sailor mumbling
        "Sea food?" into the dainty

seashell of her ear. It's just
                        as well. She finds the key,

opens the door herself,
                        and appearing in the foyer

mirror, tugs the boa tighter
                        around her Adam's apple,

checks for 5 o'clock shadow,
                        then hisses at her reflection's

smudge and smear while
                        she imagines Eduardo, Kim

Lee, and Günter combining
                        shushes into a choir to quiet

her curses, fingers to lips
                        that cost The 20th Century

more than a few bucks
                        to kiss. She sticks her tongue

out at them and reaches
                        for a banana in the fruit

bowl, rolls her eyes, and
                        puts it back among white

grapes and pomegranates.
                        She trudges to the living

room that only shadows
        crowd and grabs a pack of

Virginia Slims and a book
        of matches off the coffee

table. Wiped out by the day's
        shopping—this chicken, that

troll: her taste ageless,
        multicultural: dim sum to

Rocky Mountain oysters,
        collard greens to caviar—

she ducks out onto
        the fire escape through the bed-

room window, a rickety
        perch. A block that way:

a cathedral dome eclipses
        the setting sun; one block

the other direction,
        an observatory blocks the rising

moon. She strikes a match,
        takes a drag, its smoke

a veil, a shield, as up
        the street or down, bells chime.

When Voodoo Was *En Vogue*

6 February 1999

In his best camo—skin-tight slacks, top
four shirt buttons unbuttoned,
gold chains—
Mr. Death
could slip up behind you,
his heat rising fog-like off his skin, &

    whisk you off quick as a wink to never-
        never-lands uncharted—
           but dreamt
             of—in
          your childhood. Or
    dancing with another guy, he'd stare

his best girl-boy come-hither come-on
your way. Or leaning against
a doorway
like a
switchblade in a pawn shop
window, he'd play stud muffin for a few

    bucks or a snort or two. You'd never
    know to look at him, but
    today, I
    remember how
    the proof lay before me:
The Quilt—Mr. Death's little black book.

Sometimes the panels offer names or
names & dates, tombstones
in fabric;
other times,
just images. A candelabrum
with nine candles, five extinguished:

> a countdown: those dead & those about
> to die. On another, the last
> name of
> a dead
> man ripped off by his father,
> the hole a mouth shouting the son's

anonymity. Every panel, a wanted poster.
A bell chimes twelve times,
maybe the
National Cathedral's.
Its toll hangs in the air above
me like a flock of pigeons, not a band of

> angels bringing messages from afar.
> I want to drop to my back
> &, looking
> up, rearrange
> whitewhite clouds across
> the blueblue sky into something that

reflects what's going on here, below, or
at the very least to blindfold
the unblinking
cyclops sky.

Forty-six & smack dab in
the middle of The Quilt, I glanced around.

Few men my age. Most younger, some
much older. Against all
the odds—
not an alcoholic,
not a drug addict—I breathe,
though no one takes a breath while

others just like me have been dropping
off like flies for decades timed
to sitcom
laugh tracks,
one starring Mr. Death. Always
the exhibitionist, fresh from a Circuit

Party, still wet from shower or pool, he
wore only a white thong
as he
paraded up
& down The Quilt's avenues.
As Cass wheeled Mother Camp's chair,

he jumped onto her bony lap, scrunched
down, yelled what sounded
like *Play*
horsy &
Giddyap. Or maybe he
shouted: *A prey of divers colors, of*

needlework, colors & needlework
praying.... From this side

of The
Quilt—jigsaw
part magic, part monstrosity—
I can't remember which. Here, tourists

like me, speak the tongues of life &
death with equal ease. We
open our
mouths &
a bilingualism of cursing &
lament spills out in jingle & hymn, one

no better, no worse, than the other, but
different in the right way.
Birth to
death, our
own tracks trail us, if not
footprints or a chiffon gown's train, then

skid marks or wheel ruts laid perfectly
parallel here to Heaven
although they
meet at
the horizon, where the
world ends & you fall off—arms flailing,

mouth full of prayers & screams—into
the grinding jaws of the
unknown. In
a book
pairing names of the dead
to The Quilt's panels, I found three to

visit, & at each, I stopped, read aloud &
copied words the living
sent the
dead, lines
terse as an SOS. On the first,
a rainbow awnings a child's version of

    a tree: thirty-nine leaves, each leaf sewn
                with the name of one of
                        the dead,
                          one for
        Mike Elledge, & in the tree's
  shade, one simple poem—"Their Lives /

Graced Ours / and Their / Memories /
Nourish / Us." Later, I
found another.
His name,
Marc R. Elledge, sprawled
in cursive, white letters across red-&-

    brown stripes. I copied his poem, too:
        "and when the earth shall
                claim / your
                    limbs, then
           shall you / truly dance."
  Hours later, ready to give up, I stumbled

on Verle Dean Elledge's, his dates in
white tacked onto a strip of
black fabric.
I forgot

to copy the dates, although I
couldn't escape his photo—a relaxed

pose. His eyes found mine. To the right
of his dates, his loved ones
tacked on
patches of
his Navy stripes &, below
them, laid out his bib overalls ironed

smooth. They tucked a blue work shirt
into it, right sleeve tacked
into the
overalls' right
pocket, the left hanging to
mid-thigh. A work glove sewn onto the

cuff holds a rag or bandanna. I can't
remember which. But I can't
forget how
each article
of clothing defined him—a
uniform draped over bushes for the

night. The shirt & bibs combined, one
into one, blurred two into one
like friends
fogbound in
a jungle when nothing in
this world matters but life & death.

Coda

Though briefly popular among European royalty and aristocrats at the turn of the century, tattooing has generally been associated with marginal individuals and social groups. ...The reintroduction of tattooing in the carnival context has had a lasting impact on the way in which it has been understood in Europe and America. In the absence of an adequate appreciation for social and cultural context, tattooing tends to be regarded as aberrant entertainment provided by aliens or freaks.

—Mark C. Taylor

The Book of Toos

_____

(Write today's date here.)

Earlier today, I counted whorls
across the tips
of my fingerprints, got distracted by
a light footfall on a creaky
floorboard to my left, lost
count, began again,
got distracted by someone
clearing his
throat behind me, lost
count, began
again,
got distracted by two buddies
walking arm-in-arm,
circling the room then
circling back,
their heads close together,
whispering,
and began to count again, then one
of them or maybe both
(I couldn't tell which)
mumbled something—
Nice basket, or
Love the new do, or
We can't wait for group tonight,
can you?
—and I got distracted, lost

count, and began
again,
the one who's sometimes
nice to me, who has
soft eyes and hairy forearms,
winked, blew his
cigarette smoke against
my ear
while everyone else watched
Gilligan and the Skipper,
and I got distracted,
lost
count,
began again
began again began
again began
began
for minutes or a millennium
I couldn't tell which.

•

After all that waiting—
presto!—here I am: rush
hour, smack dab in the

middle of a city bus that's
so crowded I don't know
where my butt ends and

the next guy's begins. *A cloudless*
day, full of loss and
promise. Maybe the driver

says that or the woman
passing by on the walk.
She lugs shopping

bags and trips at the curb.
I have a plan: I get off
at the next intersection.

At the phone kiosk there,
I look up the tattoo
parlors in town but

find only one. A bum
replies, "Two blocks
thataway," pointing, and

when I get there, sure
enough, the neon calls it
Nazi Joe's Inks II Skin

just like the phone book
did. *Open,* the door's sign
says. Flash sheets curtain

the storefront window.
"There ain't no Nazi Joe,"
he says. "It's my needle

name." His eyes are pieces
                    of coal. He shaves his
                    forearms. He's 4' 8", not one

inch more, and svelte as an M-16.
                    "Just me, Leonardo,
                    but you...." He looks me

up and down. "...call me
                    Elvis." He hasn't blended
                    his rouge in. His eye

shadow's caked. He's bald
                    except for his 5 o'clock
                    shadow. He's nothing

but eyes and head. He
                    points to a hand-lettered
                    sign on the wall:

PUBLIC SKIN RESPECTED.
                    He lets me check his book
                    of tattoos. I skip each

mermaid and griffin,
                    the crucifixes and skulls,
                    thumb through page after

page of rattlers poised to
                    strike and gators with
                    wide-open chops ready

to swallow me whole, of
                panthers stalking jungles,
                spiders climbing up or

down webs, page after page
                of vows and slogans—
                Don't Tread on Me, Born

to Lose, Mommy Dearest
                —and religious
                claptrap: more Jesus

junk than at the Vatican and
                Notre Dame combined;
                666 in more versions

and variations, with more
                filigrees and curlicues
                than you could dream up

in a lifetime. "I need some
                more ink," I say. "This
                here one." I tap my

forefinger on it, a telegraph
                message. "With a few
                changes," I add. "What

you want done?" "Curl
                the bottom up like in #75
                —*A Rose Wreath to*

Remember Mother By—
> to make the curve of the
> *J.* Add Cupid's wings

from #115." I flip the pages,
> but he knows it by heart.
> "You mean *Zeus Eye-*

Balling Ganymede?" He
> adds a flourish to every
> sentence. I say, "Use the

wings as the *J*'s top" then
> ask, "How much?"
> "Hunnert bucks," he says.

"Cash," he adds. "How
> long?" I ask. "You tell
> me," he says, then

straightens up: "Coupla
> hours max. Where you
> want it?" I drop trou.

"Here," I say. "Showing
> off a might, ain't ya,
> big guy?" he says. His

rouge reddens. His eye
> shadow crinkles. "Tie me
> up and pistol-whip me,"

he says. Or maybe it's the
          DJ. He stifles a yawn. It's
          slick but practiced. He says,

"OK." He says, "It'll hurt."
          "*Shhhh*," I say, then:
          "I've been hurt worse by smaller

men than you." He laughs
          and nods. I laugh right
          back, louder, not nodding.

"Lay down," he says, "on
          your back." "Why you
          shaking?" I ask. "I always

do. One slip, I'll fuck
          it up," he admits, then
          begins to razor away hair

like a pro. He traces each
          part of the *J* onto my
          skin with a ballpoint and

hands me a mirror. I squint
          but can't tell it's patched
          together. It's that

good a job. He's biting his
          bottom lip when I hand it
          back. I hear a thud

then "Goddamn!" He's
           dropped the needle. The
           A/C's breeze knifes me

to the bone. He grunts
           when I ask, "Turn it off?"
           The ink bottles clink

together as he picks them
           up. The light above the
           table burns my eyes. I

squeeze them 'til I see
           red. Real tight like. I
           smell his sweat—days old

at least. I know there's no
           escape and want none. I
           turn my head. I still smell

him. Colored spots crawl
           across the wall like huge
           ladybugs. Before I can

ask him to dim it *humming:*
           thousands of humming-
           birds flock to my flesh,

a pointillism of hummingbirds
           blanketing my flesh,
           a whole Zodiac of

hummingbirds jabbing
> *their beaks right in,*
> *past skin, deep into*

muscle, and feed, leaving
> *a constellation*
> *across my skin,*

a stitchery, humming,
> *endorphins rushing to*
> *my brain, a swarm of*

pleasure so thick I see
> *blue behind my eyelids,*
> *not red anymore,*

my body tingling with
> *each drop of blood let—*
> I almost yell stop, but no

voice. Besides, I don't
> want him to. Pain
> swells, levels, swells

again. The humming
> swells, levels, swells
> with it. My skin's an ocean,

pain and pleasure in wave
> after wave. My skin's
> taut under his fingers.

"*Shhhh.* You're doing
                    good," he whispers, then:
                    "Glad it ain't your first time?"

and giggles. I sleep awake,
                    bridging crest and lull—
                    drop by drop—as it

mingles drop by drop—
                    with red ink, with green
                    ink, the needle humming,

Leonardo humming "Love
                    Me Tender" to himself
                    through a protective

mask (all eyes and head!),
                    dabbing blood off the
                    pinpricks with a cotton

swab in one hand, the scent
                    of alcohol rising from
                    my flesh thick as fog,

the hummingbirds humming,
                    humming, Leonardo's
                    eyes bright as flashlights

above the mask, Leonardo
                    humming, belting out a
                    word or two when he's

forgotten I'm there and
>> he's feeling confident and
>> then "Bingo!" he says,

handing me a mirror. "What'cha
>> think?" Breath catches in my
>> throat. "It pops real good,"

I say. "You're a fuckin' artiste."
>> "Why a bud and not a
>> blossom?" he asks at last.

"*Shhhh,*" I warn him,
>> raising up. He shrugs. I
>> slip my pants up over the

bandage. He recites, "It'll
>> bleed a day or two, off and
>> on. Hydrogen peroxide's

better'n alcohol." His
>> crow's-feet crinkle. I
>> think: *It must be*

tomorrow already, not
>> *today.* I hear the DJ on
>> Leonardo's transistor—

or maybe it's Leonardo—
>> say: "A cloudless day full
>> of loss or promise." I

reach into my back pocket.

"Damn," I say. "Guess what?
Someone's lifted my wallet."

Chronology and Notes

Chronology

October 31, 1946: Thomas "Buddy" Johns is born.

July 19, 1950: The narrator is born.

June 21, 1963: Buddy and the narrator's relationship begins.

November 1, 1965: Buddy enlists in the U.S. Army and begins his first and only tour of Vietnam.

December 21, 1967: The "Night of Lamentations": Buddy's death

December 24, 1967: Buddy's funeral

December 31, 1979: For the first time, the narrator is aware of being abducted by aliens; he adopts a drag persona, Cass, perhaps to escape further abductions, and meets Mother Camp.

January 1, 1980: The narrator gets The 20th Century's autograph after her last show of the evening.

October 11-13, 1996: The AIDS Memorial Quilt is displayed en total for the last time in history this weekend in Washington, DC

October 18, 1996: Mother Camp's death

December 29, 1996: The narrator visits The Wall in Washington, DC.

September 13, 1997: The 20th Century's mother is buried.

February 6, 1999: The narrator recalls visiting The Quilt with Mother Cass.

December 31, 2000: The millennium closes, according to some.

Moments ago: The narrator is released from a psychiatric ward.

Notes

—General Data—

During the U.S. government's involvement in the Vietnam "conflict," a period defined as extending from Aug. 4, 1964 to Jan. 27, 1973, approximately 47,000 U.S. citizens were killed in battle. Between 1981 and 1997, some 620,077 U. S. citizens have been identified as casualties of AIDS. (*Statistical Abstract of the United States: 1998*, pp. 367 and 147, respectively.) "The generation of men first hit by AIDS was roughly that of Vietnam veterans; thus both AIDS and the war are cast as masculine experiences in highly eroticized male-only zones." Cindy Patton, *Inventing AIDS* (New York: Routledge, 1990. 61).

Epigraph to the book: The quote by Cyrus Cassells is from "Fleur" (*Soul Make a Path Through Shouting*. Port Townsend, WA: Copper Canyon, 1994. 67-68).

—Book I: Lament for the Alien—

"La Mama Morta": The title is the title of an aria from André Chénier, music by Umberto Giordano, libretto by Luigi Illica. Andrew Beckett, the character whom Tom Hanks plays in *Philadelphia*, lip-syncs Maria Callas' recording of it.

"My Booty and Me": The snippets of lyrics from disco songs are from the following, in order of appearance: "You Sexy Thing," recorded by Hot Chocolate (1976); "Love to Love You, Baby," recorded by Donna Summer (1975); "Jungle Boogie," recorded by Kool and the Gang (1973); "Macho Man," recorded by The Village People (1978); "Boogie Nights," recorded by Heatwave (1977); "That's the Way (I Like It)," recorded by K.C. and the

Sunshine Band (1975); "Get Down Tonight," recorded by K.C. and the Sunshine Band (1975); "Le Freak," recorded by Chic (1978); and "(Shake, Shake, Shake) Shake Your Booty," recorded by K.C. and the Sunshine Band (1976).

"*Horror autotoxicus*": The phrase was coined in 1901 by German bacteriologist Paul Ehrlich and refers to "...the body's repulsion to attacking itself (for instance in auto-immune diseases). This turning upon oneself, the inability to separate self from nonself or friend from enemy, is the horror attributed to HIV." Marita Strunken, *Tangled Memories: The Vietnam War, the AIDS Epidemic, and the Politics of Remembering* (Berkeley: U. of California P., 1997. 247).

"ISO": An abbreviation meaning "in search of," it is used in sexually-oriented classified ads.

—Book II: Private Skin—
"Private skin": that part of the body usually hidden by clothing.

"A Thread Common as Breath": The phrase that begins "A prey of divers colors" is quoted from Judges 5:30 (King James Version).

—Book III: On the Shores of the River Chebar—
"The River Chebar": The prophet Ezekiel's report of his vision of the Chariot of Yahweh has been interpreted by a number of UFOlogists to be the first written account of a human being's encounter with aliens. (See Ezekiel 1.)

—Coda: The Book of Toos—
Epigraph: Mark C. Taylor, "Skinscapes," *Pierced Hearts and True*

Love: A Century of Drawings for Tattoos (New York: The Drawing Center, 1995): 30.

"Public skin": that part of the body usually not hidden by clothing (face and hands).

"Flash sheets": tattoo designs on sheets of paper.

"Needle name": a tattoo artist's nickname.

Jim Elledge's recent books include *The Chapters of Coming Forth by Day*, a prose-poem novel; *Gay, Lesbian, Bisexual, and Transgendered Myths from the Arapaho to the Zuñi*; and *Masquerade: Queer Poetry in American to the End of World War II*. His individual poems have also been published in *American Letters & Commentary*, *Court Green*, *Eleven Eleven*, *Five Fingers Review*, *Indiana Review*, *Jubilat*, *Margie*, *Paris Review*, and many other journals. Chair of the Department of English and Humanities at Pratt Institute in Brooklyn, New York, he also directs Thorngate Road, a press devoted to queer poetry.